YOU ARE SOMETHING SPECTACULAR

LET ME TELL YOU WHY

AM I YOUR BIGGEST FAN?
MAYBE. AM I AMAZED
THAT I GET TO HAVE
SOMEONE AS INCREDIBLE
AS YOU IN MY LIFE?

DEFINITELY.

LET ME TELL YOU WHY...

THIS BOOK IS A TRIBUTE
TO YOU — A TOAST TO YOUR
SPIRIT AND A TIP OF THE
HAT TO YOUR FIRE. OUT OF
THE TENS OF THOUSANDS
OF PEOPLE I'VE MET, I WANT
YOU TO KNOW — YOU'RE

I'VE FILLED THESE PAGES
WITH EVERYTHING I ADMIRE
AND APPRECIATE ABOUT YOU

(AND ALL I'M TOTALLY IN AWE OF),

BECAUSE _____ .

I PROBABLY DON'T SAY
IT ENOUGH, BUT YOU'RE

_____.

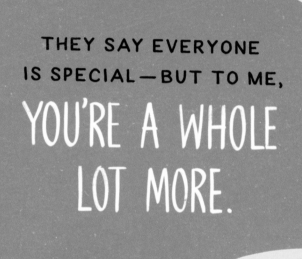

THEY SAY EVERYONE
IS SPECIAL—BUT TO ME,

YOU'RE A WHOLE
LOT MORE.

THE MOMENT I MET
YOU, I THOUGHT:

AS I GOT TO KNOW
YOU, I REALIZED:

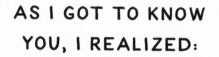

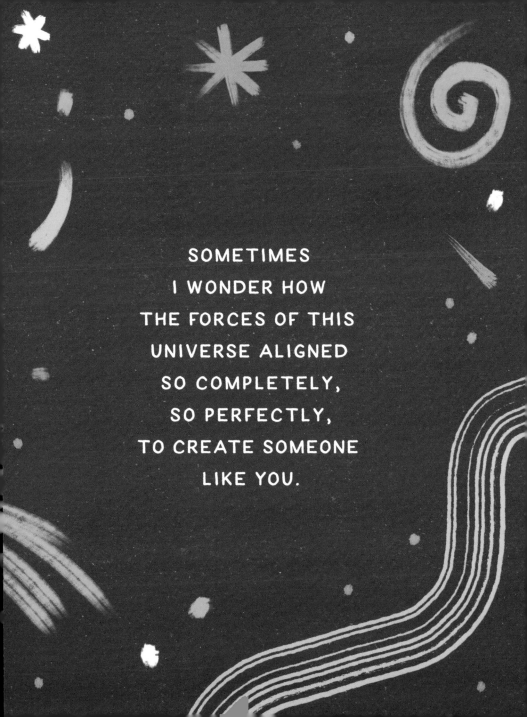

SOMETIMES
I WONDER HOW
THE FORCES OF THIS
UNIVERSE ALIGNED
SO COMPLETELY,
SO PERFECTLY,
TO CREATE SOMEONE
LIKE YOU.

YOU CHECK ALL THE BOXES FOR A
SUPER HUMAN:

PLUS, YOU CUT THROUGH
THE HUMDRUM AND MAKE

EVERY DAY

WHEREVER YOU GO, YOUR

,

, AND

SET YOU APART FROM THE CROWD.

LIKE A BRIGHT AND BRILLIANT SUN, YOU JUST RADIATE

YOU'RE ALWAYS THE

_____ PERSON

IN THE ROOM, AND THE

_____ PERSON

AT THE PARTY.

IT'S NO SURPRISE
EVERYONE YOU MEET THINKS,

"   "

THE BEST PART?

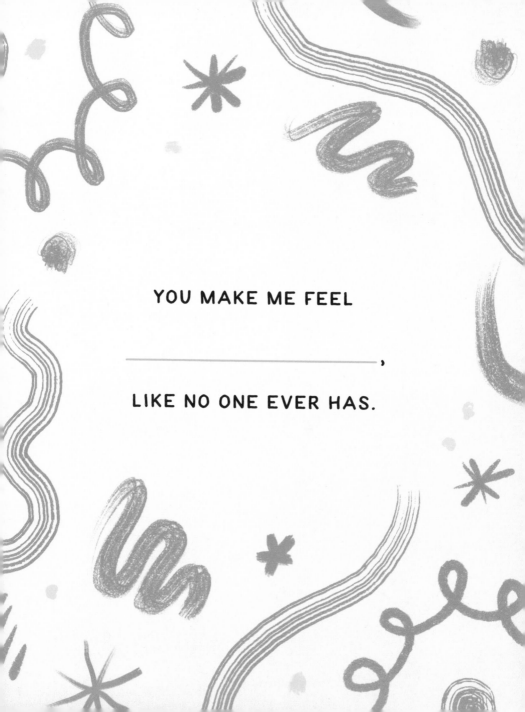

YOU MAKE ME FEEL

_____ ,

LIKE NO ONE EVER HAS.

I HAVE A THEORY THAT YOU
MUST BE SOME KIND OF

SHOOTING

STAR

HOW ELSE TO EXPLAIN YOUR
OTHERWORLDLY GIFTS?

I BRAG TO EVERYONE I KNOW
ABOUT HOW GOOD YOU ARE AT:

1

2

3

...AND I'LL FOREVER WISH
I KNEW AS MUCH ABOUT

AS YOU.

WHEN I LOOK AT YOU, I THINK,

"DANG,

"

.

...BECAUSE
YOU'VE GOT
A POWER THAT
COULD SET THE
WORLD ALIGHT.

IT'S TRUE—YOU'RE
CAPABLE OF THE MOST

MARVELOUS

AND

EXTRAORDINARY

THINGS.

YOU COULD BE A

_____ ,

A

_____ ,

OR EVEN A

_____ ,

IF YOU REALLY WANTED.

I WAS BLOWN AWAY THAT TIME YOU:

...AND I'M ALWAYS IMPRESSED WHEN YOU:

HAVE I EVER TOLD YOU?
GOOD TIMES ARE MADE
EVEN SWEETER BY YOU.

THE MEMORIES WE
SHARE ARE THE KIND
I'LL KEEP PINNED TO MY
FRIDGE FOR YEARS.

IF I COULD, I'D RELIVE
THE DAY WE:

...AND I'LL NEVER FORGET
THE TIME WE:

WHEN I'M LOST,
STUCK IN THE DARK,
OR UNSURE OF
WHAT COMES NEXT...
YOU'RE ALWAYS THERE.

LIKE THAT ONE TIME:

AND EVERY SINGLE TIME...

WHEN THINGS GET HARD AND
ANYONE ELSE WOULD CALL IT QUITS...

YOU'RE
UNSTOPPABLE

I DON'T KNOW WHAT WOULD HAVE
HAPPENED IF YOU HADN'T

NOT TO MENTION THE TIME YOU

AND TOTALLY SAVED THE DAY.

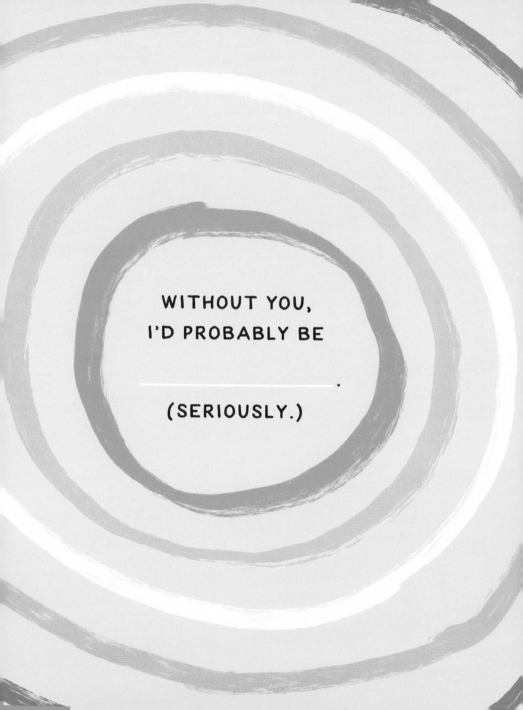

WITHOUT YOU,
I'D PROBABLY BE

_____.

(SERIOUSLY.)

YOU SHOULD
KNOW, PEOPLE AS

AS YOU SHINE A LIGHT
FOR THE REST OF US,
ILLUMINATING
WHAT'S POSSIBLE AND
SHOWING THE WAY.

ME?
I'D CONSIDER MYSELF
LUCKY
TO END UP HALF AS

AS YOU.

ALL THOSE THINGS
YOU'VE DONE FOR ME—
YOU DIDN'T HAVE TO,
BUT YOU DID ANYWAY.

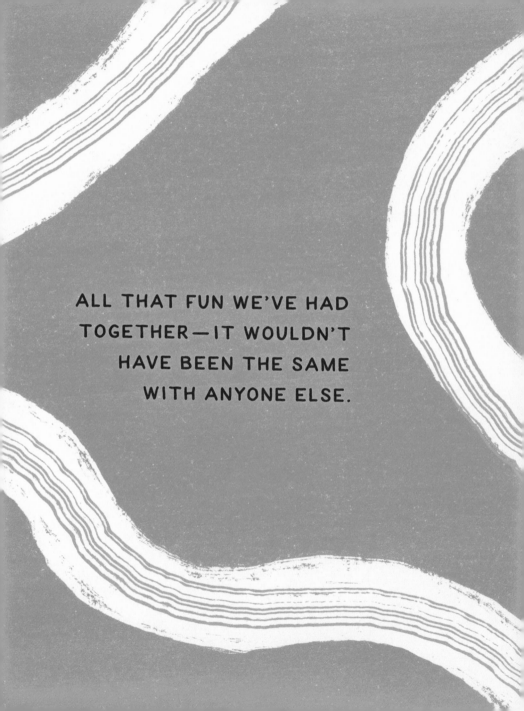

ALL THAT FUN WE'VE HAD
TOGETHER—IT WOULDN'T
HAVE BEEN THE SAME
WITH ANYONE ELSE.

I WISH I COULD THROW A

GIANT PARTY

FOR YOU, FILLED WITH YOUR
FAVORITE THINGS, LIKE

AND

(BECAUSE YOU
DESERVE IT.)

AND I WISH I COULD
TAKE YOU ON AN
ALL-EXPENSES-PAID
TRIP TO

_____ .

WE'D EAT:

DRINK:

VISIT:

AND GENERALLY HAVE
THE BEST TIME EVER.

INSTEAD,
I GIVE YOU MY

WILDEST
THANKS.

THANKS FOR
BEING TOTALLY,
COMPLETELY,
IRREPRESSIBLY

YOU.

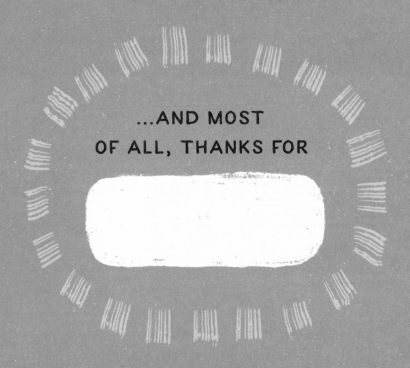

...AND MOST
OF ALL, THANKS FOR

YOU REALLY ARE

SOMETHING
SPECTACULAR.

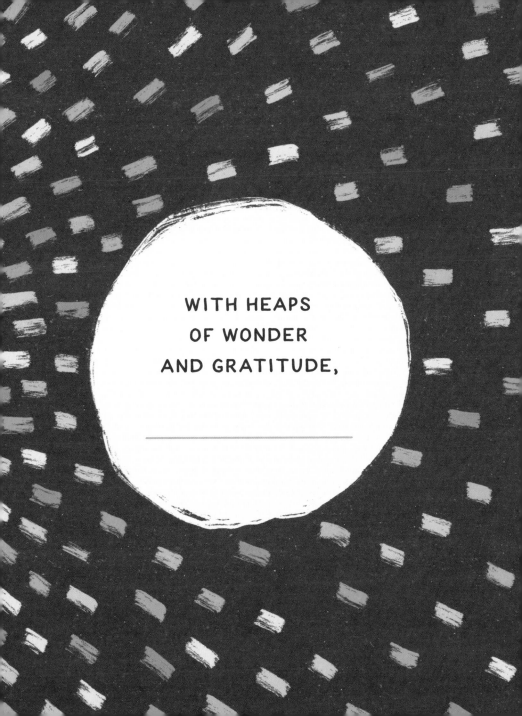

WITH HEAPS
OF WONDER
AND GRATITUDE,

_____

COMPENDIUM®
live inspired

Written by: Danielle Leduc McQueen
Designed by: Jessica Phoenix
Edited by: Amelia Riedler

ISBN: 978-1-970147-87-2

1st printing. Printed in China with soy inks on FSC®-Mix certified paper.

*Create
meaningful
moments
with gifts
that inspire.*

CONNECT WITH US
live-inspired.com | sayhello@compendiuminc.com

   @compendiumliveinspired
#compendiumliveinspired